Sensational!

Written by John Parsons

Contents	Page
Chapter 1. *Our Five Main Senses*	4
Chapter 2. *Our Sense of Sight*	6
Chapter 3. *Our Sense of Sound*	10
Chapter 4. *Our Sense of Smell*	14
Chapter 5. *Our Sense of Taste*	18
Chapter 6. *Our Sense of Touch*	22
Special Feature: *Loss of a Sense*	26
Chapter 7. *Other Senses*	28
Index and Bookweb Links	32
Glossary	Inside Back Cover

Chapter Snapshots

1. Our Five Main Senses   Page 4

When we see, hear, smell, taste, or touch things, we are using our senses to tell what is happening around us.

2. Our Sense of Sight   Page 6

Our sense of sight uses our eyes — but not all eyes are the same as ours!

IT DOESN'T LOOK MESSY TO ME!

3. Our Sense of Sound   Page 10

Our sense of sound uses our ears — but compared to many animals, we can hardly hear anything at all.

"We all share the same

4. Our Sense of Smell Page 14

There are millions of atoms in the air. Our sense of smell helps us recognize some of these atoms — like atoms from a cooked chicken or a perfume bottle.

5. Our Sense of Taste Page 18

Our tongues are covered in taste buds — but you might be surprised at how little we can taste!

6. Our Sense of Touch Page 22

How do we know if something is rough, smooth, painful, hot — or crawling down our neck? We use our sense of touch.

7. Other Senses Page 28

You may think we can sense everything with our five senses — but many animals use even more senses to give them information!

world — so watch out!"

1. Our Five Main Senses

That's sensational! When we say those words, it means that we are excited by what we can see, hear, smell, taste, or touch.

Our five main senses help our brain tell us what is happening around us.

1. We use our sense of sight through our eyes to see things.

2. We use our sense of hearing through our ears to hear sounds.

3. We use our sense of smell through our nose to smell things.

4. We use our sense of taste through our mouth to taste things.

5. We use our sense of touch through our skin to feel things.

2. Our Sense of Sight

Our sense of sight uses our eyes to collect light from the outside world.

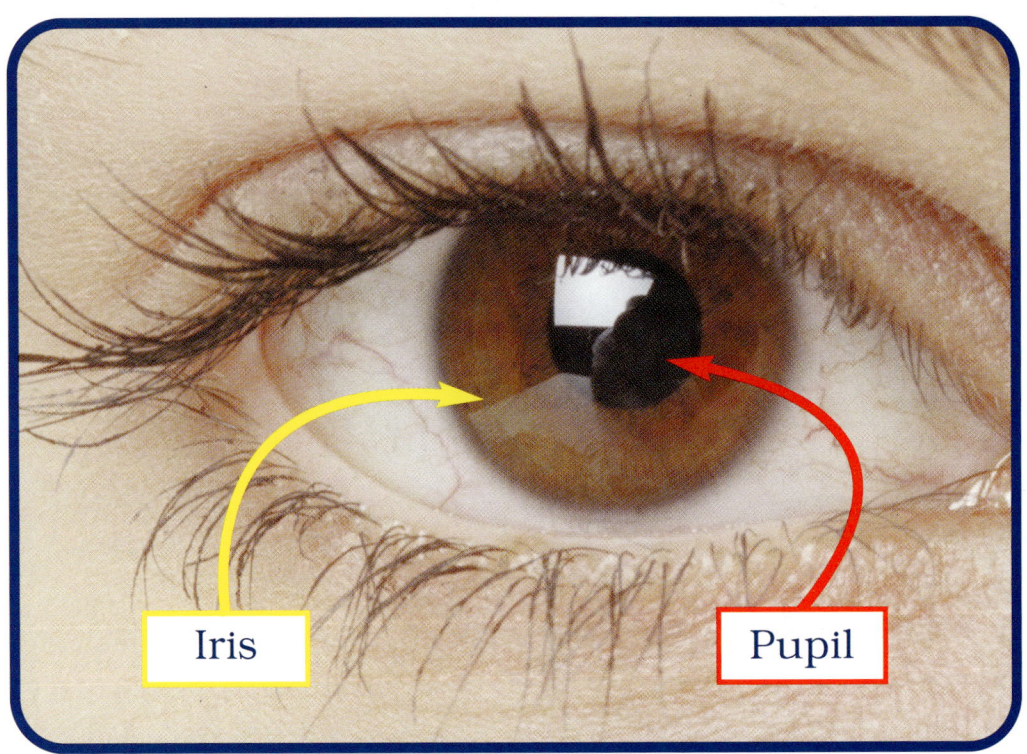

When the light is bright, the iris muscles make the pupil get smaller. This stops too much light from getting into the eye. When the light is not bright, the pupil becomes larger, and lets in more light.

Light passes through the lenses in our eyes, onto our retina. Nerves behind the retina change the information into electrical signals that are sent to the brain. A part of our brain recognizes this information as "sight." It makes a picture inside our brain of what we see around us.

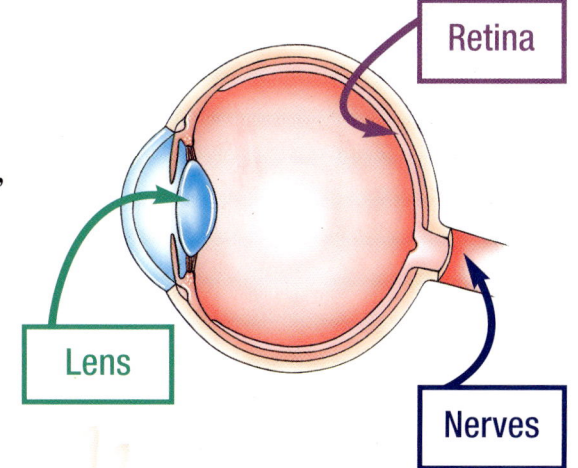

Animals' Eyes

Animals have different types of eyes for different reasons. Because cats hunt at night, their eyes let in more light. They can see things that would seem dark to us.

Cats and dogs don't need to see color, so everything looks black and white through their eyes. They do need to see movement so they can catch food in the wild. Dogs' and cats' eyes are much better than our eyes at detecting movement.

What a human can see

What a cat or dog can see

Some birds' eyes are on either side of their head. They can see two pictures in their brains at once — one from each side of their head!

Some birds, such as owls, hunt at night. They have large eyes that help them see in the dark.

Some birds, such as eagles, need to spot small animals to eat. Their eyes are much better than our eyes at spotting small things from a long distance away.

Insects' Eyes

Insects have compound eyes. Their compound eyes are made up of hundreds of tiny tubes. Each tube collects a tiny part of what they see to make a whole picture.

In this picture, the tiny circles are like the tiny tubes in compound eyes. In an insect's compound eyes, the size of the tubes are much smaller than in this picture.

3. Our Sense of Sound

Our sense of sound uses our ears to hear things. Our ears are shaped to hear many kinds of sounds. Having one ear on each side of our head helps us know where sounds are coming from.

Ears Help Our Balance

Our ears also help us sense which way is up and which way is down. This helps us keep our balance!

1. Sounds are made when things vibrate. They are called *sound vibrations*.

Boom! Boom! Boom!

2. The sound vibrations travel inside the ears until they hit the eardrums.

5. The brain recognizes this information as sound!

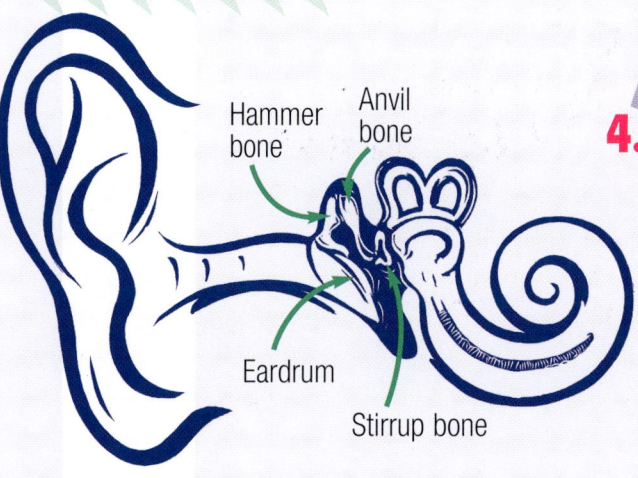

4. Nerves pick up the movement and send it as electrical information to the brain.

3. The eardrums are like thin pieces of skin, and they also vibrate when sounds hit them. Behind each eardrum, the tiny hammer, anvil, and stirrup bones move with every vibration.

Animals' Ears

People can hear many kinds of high sounds, like whistles and squeaks. People can hear many kinds of low sounds, like rumbles and thuds.

However, some animals can hear higher and lower sounds than we can.

Moving Ears

Unlike humans, many animals can move their ears to help them hear sounds better. Being able to move their ears also means animals know where the sound is coming from. This is useful if they are hunting — or being hunted!

Dolphins have the best hearing of any animals. They can hear 14 times better than we can. They communicate by making high squeaks and squealing sounds.

Bats

Bats have very poor eyesight. When bats fly around at night, they make very high squeaks that we cannot hear. Their large ears can pick up their squeaks bouncing off things in front of them. This way, they can find their way around, using sound instead of light.

Some birds, like blackbirds, can hear the low, rumbling sound of a worm moving through the soil.

Dogs can hear whistles too high for us to hear.

Cats can hear sounds so low that they can sense the sound of an earthquake!

4. Our Sense of Smell

Our sense of smell uses our nose and hairlike cells inside it to pick up and recognize the millions of smells in the air.

Atoms

The air is full of millions of smells. Each different smell is made up of many small atoms. When we open a bottle of perfume, tiny perfume atoms float into the air. When we cook a chicken, small atoms from the chicken float into the air.

Behind our nose is a large space filled with tiny hairlike cells. There are more than five million of them! Each one can recognize only one type of smell. Our brains figure out how something smells by combining all the information sent to it by these cells.

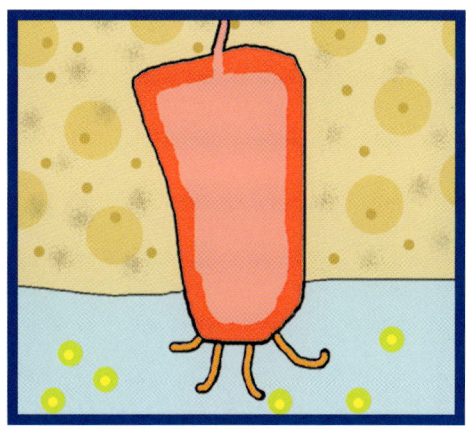

The hairlike cells are called *scent receptors*. They look like this.

15

Animals' Noses

Many animals, such as dogs, have a much better sense of smell than we do. A dog has a long nose, which means it has more room for more hairlike cells. A dog's sense of smell is about 100 times more powerful than our sense of smell.

Dogs use this sense of smell in many ways: to recognize each other, to explore the world around them, and to find smelly bones underground!

We can use a dog's great sense of smell, too. Some dogs are trained to check people's bags at airports. They can sniff for food or other things that people shouldn't bring into the country.

Many animals use their sense of smell to find each other. A moth uses its antennas to pick up smells. Male and female moths give off different smells. A male Emperor moth can find a female moth from as far away as five miles.

Protecting Fruit Trees

We can use an animal's sense of smell to control pests. Some moths are pests. They can damage fruit trees. Some fruit farmers use a spray that smells like a female moth. Every male moth around the area will fly toward the spray and become trapped. Without any males, the females cannot lay eggs. In a short time, the area will have no moths!

5. Our Sense of Taste

Our sense of taste uses the tiny taste buds on our tongue. When we eat something, our taste buds send messages along nerves to our brain.

At the same time, our sense of smell also sends messages to the brain.

Our brain combines the information from our noses and our tongues to tell us how something tastes. Our brain figures out the taste of what we are eating!

Four Tastes

Everything we eat tastes different. Or does it? Our taste buds can sense only four types of tastes:

- salty tastes
- sour tastes
- sweet tastes
- bitter tastes

Different taste buds are used to detect these tastes. They are on different parts of our tongue.

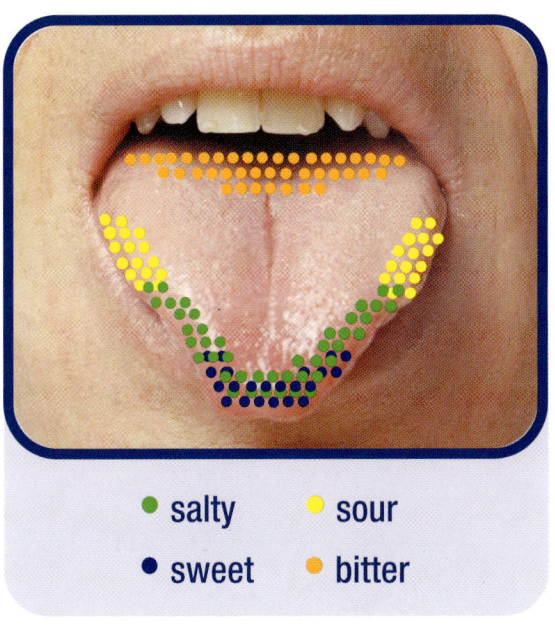

- salty
- sour
- sweet
- bitter

The salty taste buds are at the front. The sweet taste buds are at the front, too, in the center. The sour taste buds are at the sides, and the bitter taste buds are at the back of our tongue.

Your Tongue

If you look at your tongue in a mirror, it is covered in hundreds of tiny bumps. Each bump has between 100 and 200 taste buds in it!

Animals' Tongues

Animals need to taste foods, just like humans do. They need a sense of taste to know what food they like and what food they don't like. This helps them survive in their environment.

Fly Food

A fly doesn't have a tongue. Instead, it uses its feet to taste whatever food it has landed on. First, a fly will spit out a drop of liquid to dissolve some food. Then it will stand in the droplet, so its feet can tell if the food tastes good. Disgusting!

Snakes

Snakes use taste as well as sight to find their prey. They will taste the air around them by flicking their tongue around.

Tigers have a tongue with taste buds just like humans. But tigers' tongues, like all cats' tongues, have a rough, hard surface. They can use this surface like sandpaper, to remove every last piece of meat from a bone.

6. Our Sense of Touch

Our sense of touch uses tiny cells in our skin to tell us how something feels. When we touch something, those tiny cells send information to our brain. Our brain combines all the information sent to it by the skin. Then our brain figures out how something feels.

Some cells tell us if something is rough or smooth. Some cells are sensitive to heat and others to cold. Other cells can sense pain. These cells warn our brain that something is hurting us!

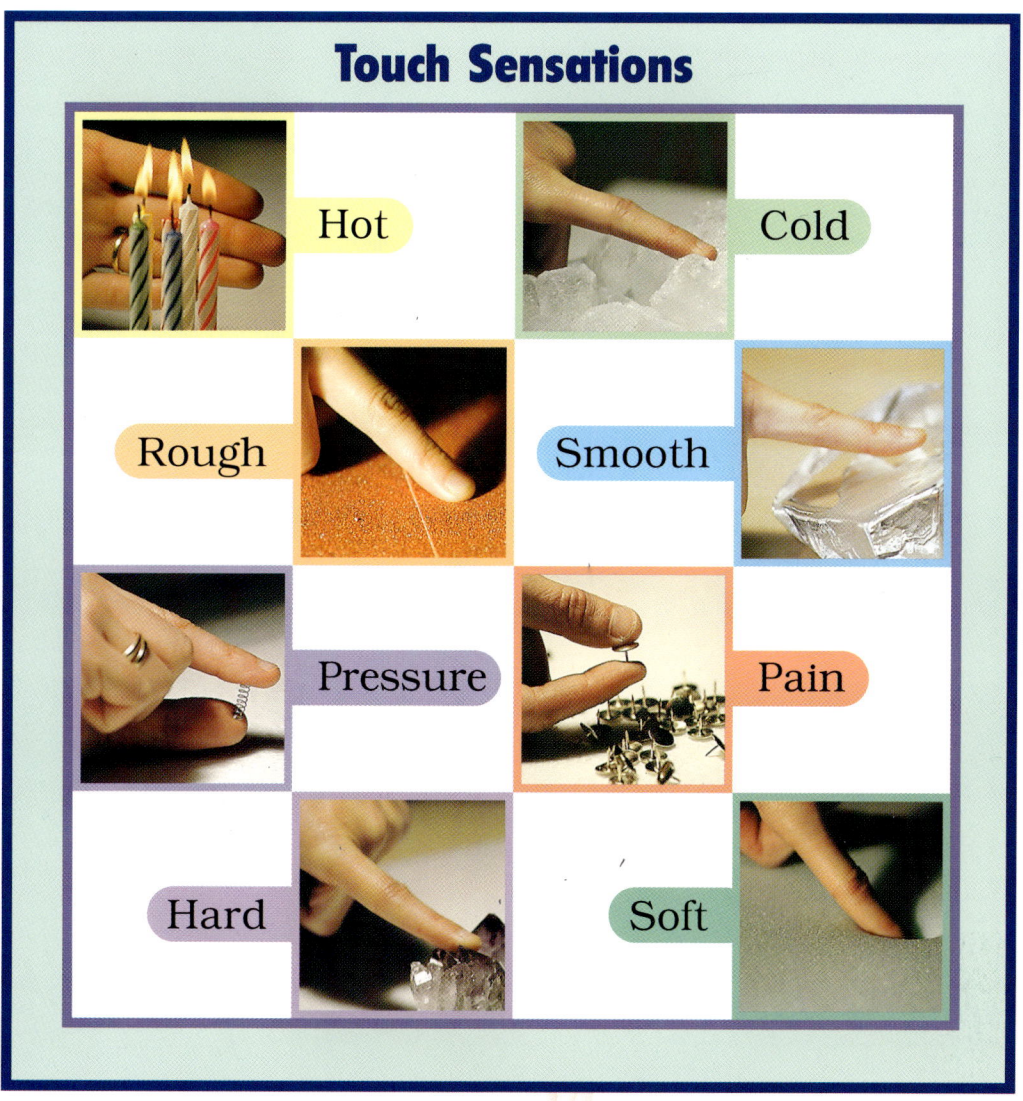

Touch Sensations

Hot · Cold · Rough · Smooth · Pressure · Pain · Hard · Soft

Certain parts of our body have more touch cells than others. They are more sensitive to touch. Our lips, tongue, fingertips, and hair roots are much more sensitive than our back.

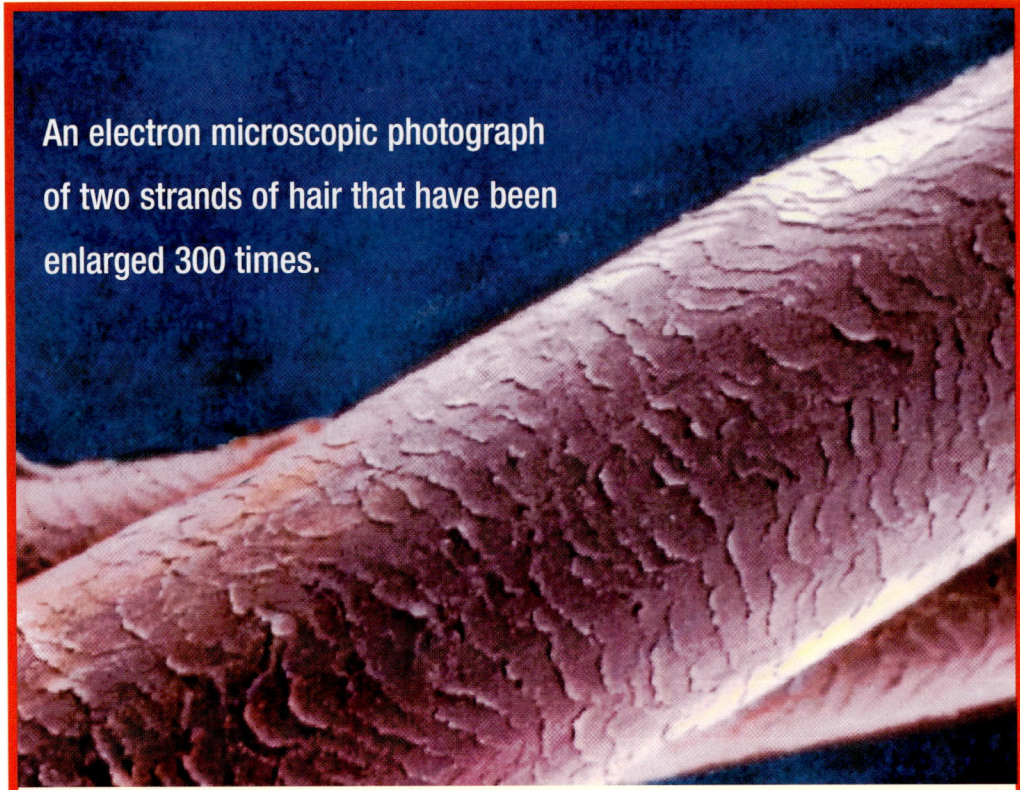

An electron microscopic photograph of two strands of hair that have been enlarged 300 times.

Hair

Hair can grow as fast as one-third of an inch per month. The average number of hairs on a person's head is between 98,000 and 120,000. People with blonde hair usually have more hairs than people with red hair!

Our lips and tongue can check how food feels. Our fingertips can check whether things are safe to handle. Movement in our hair can tell us if things around us, or on us, are moving around! This can be very helpful if an insect is crawling up our neck!

Touch and Taste

Our tongue does two jobs when it is eating. It feels the food to see if it is hot or cold or hard or soft. Then the taste buds taste it and send messages to our brain.

Some foods taste good and feel good, too. Ice cream has a lot of sugar in it, so our sweet taste buds like the taste! And it feels very cold, so it cools us down in hot weather!

Loss of a Sense

People who lose part or all of their sense of sight learn to rely on their other senses a lot more.

People who lose their sense of sight can use their sense of touch to read. Their books are printed with raised dots. These raised dots are letters called "braille." As they run their fingers over the raised letters, they can read the book!

Guide Dogs

Guide dogs are specially trained to help people who have lost their sense of sight. They guide their owners to move around safely both inside and outside their homes. Labradors make the best guide dogs. And they're great companions, too!

Nearsighted or Farsighted?

If a person can only clearly see things close-up, they are called nearsighted. If a person can only clearly see things far away, they are called farsighted. We can help the brain make clearer pictures by putting two more lenses in front of our eyes. We can wear glasses or contact lenses!

7. Other Senses

We may think we only need to use our five main senses. But those senses don't tell us all we need to know about our environment.

Ultraviolet Light

There are parts of light that we cannot see, such as ultraviolet light. This is a light that comes from the sun and can cause our skin to burn. We cannot see its colors, but some animals can. Bees can see ultraviolet light. Many flowers have ultraviolet patterns on them that help a bee find their pollen. These patterns can't be seen by people.

Animal Magnetism

Some animals may be sensitive to things like magnetism. Some scientists think that when birds such as pigeons fly long distances, they find their way by using Earth's magnetism.

Electricity in Animals

Some animals are sensitive to electricity. Many fish produce electricity and use it to find their way around solid objects. Fish have a line down the side of their body, called a lateral line. It can sense changes in electricity, pressure, and vibration.

The platypus can sense tiny amounts of electricity, too. Being able to sense electricity may help it to hunt fish!

Infrared Light

Another kind of light is infrared light. This light is made by hot objects. Infrared light cannot be seen by people. But some snakes, like rattlesnakes, have a special "eye" inside their heads. It can sense heat and infrared light. They use their infrared "sight" to sense heat from warm-blooded animals.

Protection

Animals also use their senses to protect themselves. Some insects and spiders use color to warn predators that they taste bad. Skunks spray an awful smelling liquid to escape from predators. Cats and dogs use sounds to warn other animals to keep away. Hedgehogs and porcupines use needles and spines to warn predators that they should not be touched!

Senses in Our Environment

Senses help animals and people live together in the same environment. Each use their senses to eat, to move around, or to keep safe. That's why the world may look different through the eyes of animals and people. But we all share the same world — so watch out! You never know who or what might be watching, listening, smelling, touching, or licking their lips right now!

Index

atoms 14
balance 10
bats 13
birds 9, 13, 28
braille 27
brain 5, 7, 11, 15, 18, 22
cats 8, 13, 21, 30
cells 14–16, 22–24
compound eyes 9
dogs 8, 13, 16, 26, 30
dolphins 12
eagles 9
ears 5, 10-13
electricity 29
eyes 5, 6-9
fly 20
hair 24–25
hearing aid 27
infrared light 29
insects 9, 30
lenses 7, 27
magnetism 28
moth 17
nerves 7, 11
nose 14–17
owls 9
pests 17
retina 7
scent receptor 15
snakes 20, 29
sound vibrations 11
taste buds 19
tiger 20
tongue 18–21, 24–25
ultraviolet light 28

Bookweb Links

Read more Bookweb 3 books about how we use senses in our environment:

Detector Dog — Nonfiction
Optometrist — Nonfiction
Instrument Families — Nonfiction
The Dog's Guide to Humans — Fiction
Mr. Florentine's Violin — Fiction
Inspector Grub and the Jelly Bean Robber — Fiction

Key To Bookweb Fact Boxes
☐ Arts
☐ Health
☐ Science
☐ Social Studies
☐ Technology